Sounds

Contents

Written by Julie Sykes
Photography by Martin Sookias

Collins

CW00951105

Hearing sounds

You hear sounds with your ears.
There are sounds all around you.

bang

boom

buzz

hum

ding-dong

Which sounds do you like?

buzzz

bbbbrrrrring

SMASH

3

Making sounds

Sounds are made in many ways.

The clapper hits the bell and the bell makes a sound.

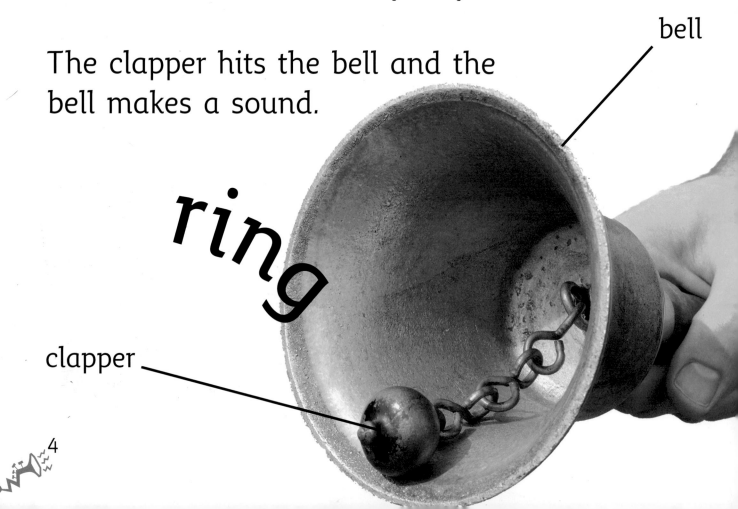

bell

ring

clapper

There are little bells and big bells.

A church bell

A bicycle bell

The drumstick hits the drum and the drum makes a sound.

drumstick

bang-bang-a-boom!

drum

Some drums are big and some are small.

You pluck a string and it makes a sound.

twang

string

8

You blow into a recorder and it makes a sound.

toot

toot

toot

9

Loud and soft sounds

Some sounds are soft ...

whisper whisper

... and some sounds are loud.
Loud sounds can hurt your ears.

drrrrrr!

11

Sounds all around

Listen to the sounds
around you.
Can you tell what's
making them?

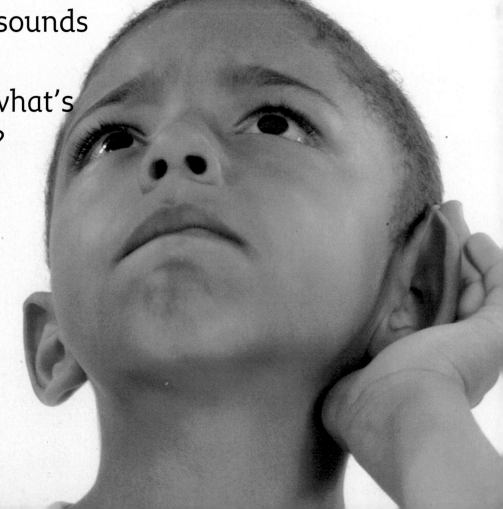

ROAR

pheep

13

Sounds index

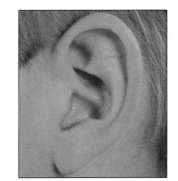

Ideas for guided reading

Learning objectives: discuss content of the text showing precise understanding; solve new words using print information and meaning; use the words fiction and non-fiction appropriately; understand the purpose of contents and index pages; know new words from reading and make collections of words linked to topics; take turns to speak.

Curriculum links: Science: Ourselves (the five senses); Sound and hearing

High frequency words: some, like, many, ways, this, makes, if

Interest words, clapper, bell, drum, stick, ears, sound, loud, soft, guitar, recorder, string, blow, pluck

Word count: 109

Getting started

- Give out some instruments, e.g. bells, drums and recorders. Ask the children to play them making loud and quiet sounds.

- Play a listening game where children guess the instrument sounds with their eyes shut. Discuss the verbs appropriate to playing instruments, e.g. blowing, plucking, banging and shaking.

- Show the children the front and back covers and read the title and blurb. Walk through the text and ask children to discuss the pictures and what is happening in them.

- Write the names of some of the instruments on the whiteboard and ask the children to find the instruments in the text.

Reading and responding

- Ask children to read the book aloud and independently up to p12. Observe, prompt and praise children for speedy self-correction, for using pictures to aid reading and for reading fluently without pointing at words.

- Ask them to read the different sound words (*bang, buzz, ring*) with expression. When they reach p12, ask them to listen to sounds around them. Ask them in turn what other sounds they can hear.